D1254715

MAKE IT YOURSELF!

COLLAGES &
SCULPTURES

Carol Hove

**Checkerboard
Library**

An Imprint of Abdo Publishing
abdopublishing.com

abdopublishing.com

Published by Abdo Publishing, a division of ABDO, PO Box 398166, Minneapolis, Minnesota 55439. Copyright © 2018 by Abdo Consulting Group, Inc. International copyrights reserved in all countries. No part of this book may be reproduced in any form without written permission from the publisher. Checkerboard Library™ is a trademark and logo of Abdo Publishing.

Printed in the United States of America, North Mankato, Minnesota
062017
092017

THIS BOOK CONTAINS
RECYCLED MATERIALS

Design: Sarah DeYoung, Mighty Media, Inc.
Production: Mighty Media, Inc.
Editor: Liz Salzmann
Cover Photographs: Mighty Media, Inc.
Interior Photographs: iStockphoto; Mighty Media, Inc.; Shutterstock

The following manufacturers/names appearing in this book are trademarks: Craft Smart®, Crayola®, Johnson®, LaCroix®, MagTray™, Mod Podge®, Sharpie®, 3M™

Publisher's Cataloging-in-Publication Data
Names: Hove, Carol, author.
Title: Make it yourself! collages & sculptures / by Carol Hove.
Other titles: Make it yourself! collages and sculptures I Collages and
    sculptures
Description: Minneapolis, MN : Abdo Publishing, 2018. I Series: Cool
    makerspace I Includes bibliographical references and index.
Identifiers: LCCN 2016962471 I ISBN 9781532110672 (lib. bdg.) I
    ISBN 9781680788525 (ebook)
Subjects: LCSH: Makerspaces--Juvenile literature. I Handicraft--
    Juvenile literature.
Classification: DDC 680--dc23
LC record available at http://lccn.loc.gov/2016962471

TO ADULT HELPERS

This is your chance to assist a new maker! As children learn to use makerspaces, they develop new skills, gain confidence, and make cool things. These activities are designed to help children create projects in makerspaces. Children may need more assistance for some activities than others. Be there to offer guidance when they need it. Encourage them to do as much as they can on their own. Be a cheerleader for their creativity.

Before getting started, remember to lay down ground rules for using tools and supplies and for cleaning up. There should always be adult supervision when using a hot or sharp tool.

SAFETY SYMBOLS

Some projects in this book require the use of hot or sharp tools. That means you'll need some adult help for these projects. Determine whether you'll need help on a project by looking for these safety symbols.

HOT!
This project requires the use of a hot tool.

SHARP!
This project requires the use of a sharp tool.

CONTENTS

What's a MAKERSPACE?

Can you imagine a crafting space filled with art supplies? Scissors, crayons, paper, and more are all within reach! The area is buzzing with the activity and creativity of other crafters like you.

This is a makerspace. It is an area where people come together to create all kinds of cool stuff. Makers share sparks of creativity. They love to learn something new. They work together to design and create wonderful **collages** and sculptures. Are you ready to become a maker?

FUN WITH COLLAGES & SCULPTURES

Materials are a very important part of a successful maker project. Creativity is also important. Let the supplies provided in your makerspace determine how you will create a project.

Some projects will call for certain supplies. But don't worry if you are missing some materials. The best makers are problem-solvers, so use your imagination! Find another item to substitute for the missing one.

COLLAGE & SCULPTURE TIPS

Sharing is an important aspect of a makerspace. Makers share workspace, materials, and ideas. Being surrounded by other makers is great for creativity. But it also means a lot of projects may be happening at once. Here are some tips for successful makerspace projects.

HAVE A PLAN

Read through a project before beginning. Research any terms you may not know. Make sure you have everything you need for the project.

ASK FOR PERMISSION

Get **permission** from an adult to use the space, tools, and supplies.

BE RESPECTFUL

Before taking a tool or material, make sure another maker isn't using it.

KEEP YOUR SPACE CLEAN

Collage and sculpture materials can be messy. Protect surfaces with newspaper to make cleanup easier. Wear old clothes or an apron that you're allowed to get stained.

EXPECT MISTAKES & BE CREATIVE!

Being a maker isn't about creating something perfect. Have fun as you work!

SUPPLIES

Here are some of the materials and tools you'll need to do the projects in this book.

acrylic paint

aluminum foil

aluminum soda cans

chenille stems

craft knife

craft sticks

decorative paper

double-sided tape

drill & drill bits

duct tape

felt

googly eyes

hammer

hot glue gun & glue sticks

Mod Podge

nails

needle-nose pliers

paint pens

sandpaper

stretched
canvas

tissue paper

wooden
dowels

COLLAGE & SCULPTURE TECHNIQUES

To open chains or parts of metal pieces, hold each side with a needle-nose pliers. Twist the ends apart. Then twist the other way to close.

To tear tissue paper, run a moist cotton swab where you want to rip the paper. Gently tear the paper while it is wet. Let the paper dry.

THE NAME GAME

Craft your name in cool collage letters!

WHAT YOU NEED

newspaper

wooden letters

paint

paintbrush

cardboard

marker

decorative items (game pieces & small toys)

craft glue

hot glue gun & glue sticks

10

1. Cover your work surface with newspaper. Paint the letters. Let them dry.

2. Trace around each letter on a piece of cardboard.

3. Arrange the decorative items on the cardboard letters. Play around with the design until you are happy with it. Layer the items for a **3-D** look.

4. Glue the pieces onto the wooden letters. Use craft glue for light, flat pieces. Use hot glue for heavier items. Let the glue dry.

 **TIP** Instead of using wooden letters, try cutting the letters out of cardboard.

FREE-FORM FOIL ART

Turn junk into a fabulous foil masterpiece.

WHAT YOU NEED

sturdy cardboard

string

small objects
(not too thick or bulky)

craft glue

hot glue gun & glue sticks

aluminum foil

paint

paintbrush

paper towels

1. Arrange some string and other objects on the cardboard. Glue the objects in place.

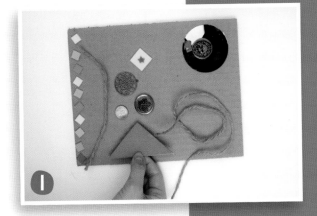

2. Tear off a sheet of aluminum foil large enough to cover the cardboard. Press the foil firmly over the objects. Start in the center and work toward the edges.

3. Wrap the extra foil to the back of the cardboard.

4. Add color with paint. Let the paint dry a little bit. Then dab and smear it with paper towels to create an interesting color effect.

5. Let the paint dry completely.

CRAYON MOSAIC

Build a beautiful mini mural
out of colorful crayons!

WHAT YOU NEED

pencil

stretched canvas

crayons

craft knife

hot glue gun & glue
sticks

14

1. Sketch a design on the canvas.

2. Select the crayon colors you need. Peel the labels off the crayons.

3. Arrange pieces of crayon row by row to fill in the design. Carefully use a craft knife to cut the crayon pieces as needed.

4. Use the hot glue to attach each crayon piece. Let the glue dry.

 **TIP** Use the craft knife to cut the crayon wrappers. This makes the wrappers easier to remove.

FUNKY METAL WIND CHIME

Mix metal objects to create a cheerful chime to jingle in the wind.

1. Gather an assortment of metal objects. These can include old kitchen **utensils**, small tools, keys, chains, nuts, washers, and springs.

2. Choose an object for the top to hang the wind chime elements from.

3. Arrange the objects in vertical rows. You could make human figures or **abstract** arrangements.

4. Connect the objects in each row. Some items may have clips or chain links to connect them with. Otherwise, connect the objects with pieces of wire.

5. Connect each row to the top piece.

6. Find a great spot outside to hang up your chime!

PAPER COLLAGE

Let your imagination lead the way as you craft this cool collage.

WHAT YOU NEED

newspaper • stretched canvas • acrylic paint
round paintbrush • tissue paper
decorative paper • scissors • paper punches
Mod Podge • smooth, wide paintbrush

1. Cover your work surface with newspaper. Paint a light border around the edges of the canvas.

2. Paint the sides of the canvas.

3. Tear or cut paper into small pieces. Use different colors, shapes, and patterns. Try using paper punches to make shapes. Anything goes!

4. Use a smooth, wide paintbrush to brush Mod Podge on a small area of the canvas. Place a piece of paper on the Mod Podge. Brush more Mod Podge over the piece of paper.

5. Add more pieces of paper the same way. Overlap the pieces until the canvas is completely covered.

6. Brush a layer of Mod Podge over the entire canvas. Let it dry. Add a second layer of Mod Podge. Let it dry.

COMMUNITY COLLAGE

Create an art project where everyone gets to show their style!

WHAT YOU NEED

newspaper

large cardboard box

paint

paintbrush

colorful duct tape

decorative items (pushpins, computer parts, buttons, figurines, paper, paint chips, wood pieces, anything else)

hot glue gun & glue sticks

craft glue

double-sided tape

1. Cover your work surface with newspaper. Paint the box a solid color. Let it dry.

2. Tape the box closed with colorful duct tape.

3. Put the box and the decorative items in a makerspace that is open to many people. Be sure to include craft glue, hot glue, and double-sided tape.

4. Invite people to use their creativity and add decorations to the box.

 TIP Make a sign to let people know about the project. Invite them to bring their own items to add, or use what is provided in the makerspace.

CAN CRITTER SCULPTURE

Craft some cute critters to keep you company.

WHAT YOU NEED

4 empty aluminum soda cans • shoes • paint pens

patterned duct tape • leather or felt • scissors • hot glue gun & glue sticks

googly eyes • chenille stems • 20-inch (50 cm) board • sandpaper • ruler

pencil • drill & drill bits • newspaper • paint • paintbrush • 4 wooden dowels

1. Bend a can so the bottom faces one way and the top faces the other way. Step on the can to flatten it. Wear shoes when you do this so you don't cut your foot.

2. Use a paint pen to color in the bottom of the can. Let it dry. This is the critter's snout.

3. Cover the rest of the can with duct tape. This is the animal's head.

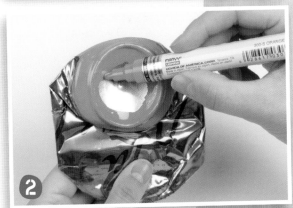

4. Cut ears out of leather or felt. Glue them to the back of the face so they stick out.

Continued on the next page.

5 Create more features with googly eyes, felt, leather, and chenille stems. Tape or glue them to the head.

6. Repeat steps 1 through 5 to make three more critters.

7 Sand the board until it is smooth. This is the base.

8 Make four marks down the center of the base. Space them about 5½ inches (14 cm) apart.

9. Have an adult help you drill a hole at each mark. Use a drill bit the same size as the dowels.

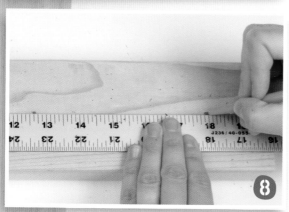

10. Cover your work surface with newspaper. Paint the base a solid color. Let it dry.

11. Decorate the base with paint pens. Let the paint dry.

12. Cut the dowels to between 8 and 12 inches (20 and 30 cm). They can each be a slightly different length. Paint the dowels fun colors. Let the paint dry.

13. Lay the end of a dowel on the back of each animal. Use duct tape or hot glue to secure the dowels.

14. Stick the dowels into the holes in the base. If needed, use hot glue to hold the dowels in position.

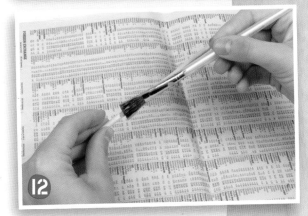

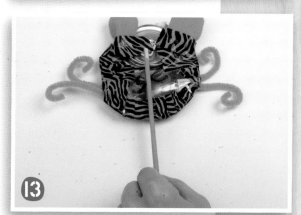

CARDBOARD CITYSCAPE

Let your imagination take you to faraway places as you build the city of your dreams!

WHAT YOU NEED

variety of boxes • camera • newspaper • paint • paintbrush

paint pens • markers • cardboard scraps • scissors

hot glue gun & glue sticks • pencil • craft knife • colored paper

craft sticks • craft glue • 2 large nails • hammer

1. Arrange the boxes to form a **cityscape**.

2. Take a picture of your cityscape. This will help you remember the arrangement.

3. Cover your work surface with newspaper. Paint the boxes. Solid-colored boxes may not need to be painted.

4. Use paint pens and markers to draw doors directly on some buildings.

5. Cut other doors out of cardboard. Paint the doors in colors that go with the buildings. Use markers and paint pens to draw detail on the doors. Hot glue the doors to the buildings.

Continued on the next page.

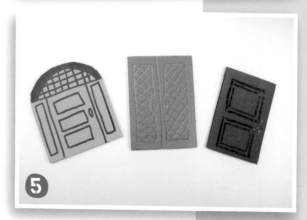

6. Use paint pens and markers to draw windows directly on some of the buildings.

7 Cut other windows out of cardboard. Add detail to the windows with paint pens and markers. Hot glue the windows to the buildings.

8 Try making a box window. Use a pencil to draw the window frame on a small box. Carefully cut out the window panes with a craft knife. Paint the window frame. Hot glue the box window to a building.

9 Hot glue the boxes together to create your **cityscape**. Use the picture you took to remember where each one goes.

10. Use a nail to poke two holes in the back of the cityscape. Make sure the holes are at the same height. Have an adult help you use the nails to hang the cityscape on a wall.

BRIGHT IDEA!

Add more details to make your **cityscape** come to life!

- **Accordion-fold** a piece of paper. Glue it over a window for an **awning**. Or make awnings out of cardboard.

- Make a clock tower. Cut a square out of cardboard. Cut out a triangle that fits on top of the square. Paint all the cardboard pieces. Print out or draw a clock face that fits on the square. Hot glue the pieces to a building.

- Glue craft sticks together to make a fence. Let the glue dry. Paint the fence. Hot glue it to the cityscape.

PLAN A MAKER EVENT!

Being a maker is not just about the finished product. It is about communication, **collaboration**, and creativity. Do you have a project you'd like to make with the support of a group? Then make a plan and set it in action!

SECURE A SPACE

Think of places that would work well for a makerspace. This could be a library, school classroom, or space in a community center. Then, talk to adults in charge of the space. Describe your project. Tell them how you would use the space and keep it organized and clean.

INVITE MAKERS

Once you have a space, it is time to spread the word! Work with adults in charge of the space to determine how to do this. You could make an e-invitation, create flyers about your maker event, or have family and friends tell others.

MATERIALS & TOOLS

Materials and tools cost money. How will you supply these things? **Brainstorm** ways to raise money for your makerspace. You could plan a fund-raiser to buy needed items. You could also ask makers to bring their own supplies.

GLOSSARY

abstract — in art, expressing ideas or emotions without attempting to create a realistic picture.

accordion-fold — to fold back and forth like the sides of an accordion.

awning — a rooflike structure, usually canvas, that provides protection.

brainstorm — to come up with a solution by having all members of a group share ideas.

cityscape — an artistic representation of a city.

collaboration — the act of working with another person or group in order to do something or reach a goal.

collage — art composed of a variety of materials, such as paper and cloth, glued onto a surface.

permission — when a person in charge says it's okay to do something.

three-dimensional (3-D) — having length, width, and height and taking up space.

utensil — a tool, such as a spoon, used for a particular purpose.

WEBSITES

To learn more about Cool Makerspace, visit **abdobooklinks.com**. These links are routinely monitored and updated to provide the most current information available.

INDEX